READY, STEADY, PRACTISE!

Paul Broadbent

Mental Arithmetic
Pupil Book Year 6

Features of this book

- Clear explanations and worked examples for each mental arithmetic topic from the KS2 National Curriculum.

- Questions split into three sections that become progressively more challenging:

Warm up

Test yourself

Challenge yourself

- 'How did you do?' checks at the end of each topic for self-evaluation.

- Regular progress tests to assess pupils' understanding and recap on their learning.

- Answers to every question in a pull-out section at the centre of the book.

Contents

Numbers and place value

One more than 999 999 is 1 million.

1 million is written as 1 000 000.

Use this table to help you read numbers greater than 1 million.

Millions			Thousands			Ones		
hundreds	tens	units	hundreds	tens	units	hundreds	tens	units
		6	8	4	3	9	1	8

6 843 918 is read as 6 **million** 843 **thousand** 918.

6 000 000 + 800 000 + 40 000 + 3000 + 900 + 10 + 8 = 6 843 918

Warm up

1 Write each number in numerals.

a) six million four hundred thousand nine hundred and twenty-six

b) nine million two hundred and eighteen thousand and seventy-four

c) two million one hundred thousand

d) three million two hundred and ninety thousand five hundred and ninety-one

e) one million four hundred thousand two hundred and twelve

f) four million one thousand three hundred and ninety

g) seven million two thousand and eight

h) one million four hundred thousand two hundred and sixty

2 Write each of these numbers in words.

a) 6 785 141

b) 1 510 930

3 Copy and circle the correct digit in each number to match the value.

> **Example:** 2 0 6 7 ③ 9 5   three hundred

a) 2 9 6 9 9 2 1   nine hundred thousand

b) 7 2 2 4 0 2 5   twenty thousand

c) 3 3 6 3 2 8 0   three million

d) 8 5 5 0 1 5 9 7   five hundred thousand

Challenge yourself

4 Here are the approximate populations of some of the largest cities in the world. Draw a table like the one below and write the cities in order of population, starting with the largest.

Cairo (Egypt) 15 837 460

Mexico City (Mexico) 22 843 550

Moscow (Russia) 14 432 190

Shanghai (China) 16 708 510

London (UK) 12 412 330

Mumbai (India) 19 463 950

New York (USA) 22 310 740

Tokyo (Japan) 35 521 740

City	Country	Population

How did you do?

Negative numbers

All whole numbers are called **integers**. Integers can be positive or negative. Zero is an integer.

Remember the following:

- When you move left on a number line, numbers get smaller.
- When you move right on a number line, numbers get larger.

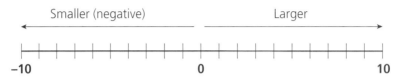

Smaller (negative) — Larger

−10   0   10

1 What number does each arrow point to?

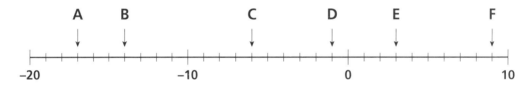

A   B   C   D   E   F

−20   −10   0   10

Test yourself

2 Look at the number line in question 1. What is the difference between:

a) **A** and **D**?   b) **C** and **E**?

c) **B** and **F**?   d) **E** and **B**?

3 Write these temperatures in order, starting with the lowest.

18°C   −13°C   −14°C   0°C   3°C   −5°C

4 What is the difference in temperature between these pairs of thermometers?

a)

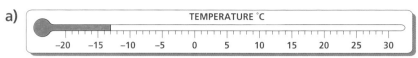

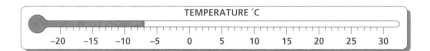

b)

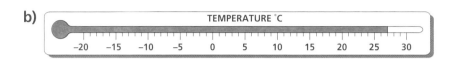

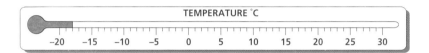

c)

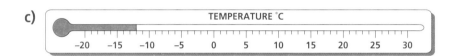

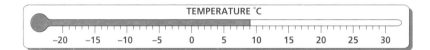

Challenge yourself

5 Rashid was trying to roll a marble on to a target line of exactly 1 metre.
He recorded each attempt in centimetres above or below his target.

1st	2nd	3rd	4th	5th	6th	7th	8th
+6	+1	−4	−7	−2	0	+2	−3

a) What was the length of his longest roll?

b) What was the length of his shortest roll?

c) On which attempt did he land on the target line?

d) On which attempt did he roll 97 cm?

e) How would he have recorded a roll of 94 cm?

How did you do?

Order of operations

If a calculation involves brackets, then the calculation must be done in the following order:

Brackets

Division

Multiplication

Addition

Subtraction

Example:

$5 \times (3 + 8) - 2$ ← Brackets first,

$= 5 \times 11 - 2$ ← no division, so now multiply,

$= 55 - 2$ ← no addition, so now subtract

$= 53$

Compare these to see how important brackets are:

$26 - (5 + 12) = 9$

$(26 - 5) + 12 = 33$

$(12 \div 4) + 2 = 5$

$12 \div (4 + 2) = 2$

Warm up

1. Answer these calculations.

   a) $(27 - 13) + 4 =$ b) $54 - (17 + 12) =$

   c) $(23 - 15) \times 2 =$ d) $52 - (28 - 19) =$

   e) $3 \times (29 - 18) =$ f) $(12 + 36) \div 2 =$

   g) $(48 + 6) - (12 \times 3) =$ h) $(9 \times 4) \div (22 - 16) =$

Test yourself

2. Copy and add brackets in the correct places to make these calculations correct.

   a) $5 - 3 \times 4 + 2 = 12$

   b) $15 + 21 \div 7 - 8 = 10$

   c) $9 \div 3 + 6 - 5 = 4$

   d) $2 \times 4 + 2 \times 4 = 48$

   e) $5 + 10 - 18 \div 9 = 13$

3 What are the missing numbers?

a) (__ × 4) − 1 = 11

b) 10 − (__ × 3) = 4

c) (4 × 2) + (__ × 3) = 17

d) (__ × 5) − (5 × 4) = 10

e) 12 ÷ (__ × 2) = 2

Challenge yourself

4 Write calculations to complete this table.

Use only the numbers 2, 4, 5, 6 and 8 and any operation (+, −, ×, ÷).

Can you find different ways to make the numbers 1 to 20? Try to use brackets for each one.

Example: (5 + 8) − (2 × 6) = 1

1 ⟶	11 ⟶
2 ⟶	12 ⟶
3 ⟶	13 ⟶
4 ⟶	14 ⟶
5 ⟶	15 ⟶
6 ⟶	16 ⟶
7 ⟶	17 ⟶
8 ⟶	18 ⟶
9 ⟶	19 ⟶
10 ⟶	20 ⟶

How did you do?

Addition and subtraction

When you add two numbers mentally, you can add to one of the numbers, as long as you subtract the same amount from the other number.

Example:

$$68 + 73 \longrightarrow \begin{array}{l} 68 + \mathbf{2} = \mathbf{70} \\ 73 - \mathbf{2} = \mathbf{71} \end{array} \longrightarrow 70 + 71 = 141$$

When you subtract two numbers mentally, you can add to or subtract from one of the numbers, as long as you do the same to the other number.

Example:

$$113 - 87 \longrightarrow \begin{array}{l} 113 + \mathbf{3} = \mathbf{116} \\ 87 + \mathbf{3} = \mathbf{90} \end{array} \longrightarrow 116 - 90 = 26$$

Warm up

1 Add these mentally. Use the method shown above if it helps.

a) 59 + 86 =   b) 67 + 48 =

c) 83 + 98 =   d) 107 + 76 =

e) 119 + 104 =   f) 154 + 191 =

2 Subtract these mentally. Use the method shown above if it helps.

a) 83 − 57 =   b) 76 − 48 =

c) 94 − 76 =   d) 125 − 49 =

e) 154 − 87 =   f) 143 − 105 =

3 Look at the numbers below. Find pairs of numbers that total 8500.

3800   4800   2900   4700   3900   4600   3700   5600

4 Copy and complete these.

+	89	168
134		
215		

+	203	
169		597
	527	

+		109
		686
438	826	

Challenge yourself

5 Investigate this problem, called 'Kaprekar's Constant'.

- Take any three digits that are not all identical.
- Rearrange the digits to form the largest and smallest three-digit numbers possible.
- Subtract the smaller number from the larger.
- Take the answer and repeat the above process, making the smallest and largest possible numbers and finding the difference.
- Repeat this again and again.

What number do you end up with?

Example:

4 3 6

The largest three-digit number is 643 and the smallest is 346.

643 – 346 = 297
972 – 279 = 693
963 – 369 = 594
954 – 459 = 495
954 – 459 = 495

Multiplication

When you multiply tenths by a whole number, change the tenth to a whole number (by multiplying by 10), multiply the two numbers and then divide the answer by 10.

Example: What is 0.8 × 3?

$$0.8 \times 10 = 8$$
$$8 \times 3 = 24$$
$$24 \div 10 = 2.4$$
$$\text{So } 0.8 \times 3 = 2.4$$

When you multiply decimals greater than 1, break the decimal number into the whole number and tenth. Multiply each part then add the two numbers together.

Example: What is 1.7 × 5?

$$1.7 \times 5 = (1 \times 5) + (0.7 \times 5)$$
$$= 5 + 3.5$$
$$= 8.5$$

Warm up

1 Answer these calculations.

a) 8 × 5 =

0.8 × 5 =

b) 3 × 7 =

0.3 × 7 =

c) 9 × 4 =

0.9 × 4 =

d) 7 × 6 =

0.7 × 6 =

e) 8 × 8 =

0.8 × 8 =

f) 7 × 9 =

0.7 × 9 =

g) 7 × 7 =

0.7 × 7 =

h) 9 × 5 =

0.9 × 5 =

2 Copy and complete these.

a) 4.3 × 5 = (4 × 5) + (0.3 × 5)

= _____ + _____

= _____

b) 7.5 × 8 = (____ × ____) + (____ × ____)

= _____ + _____

= _____

c) 8.6 × 9 = (____ × ____) + (____ × ____)

= _____ + _____

= _____

d) 5.9 × 3 = (____ × ____) + (____ × ____)

= _____ + _____

= _____

e) 6.2 × 7 = (____ × ____) + (____ × ____)

= _____ + _____

= _____

Challenge yourself

3 Use the digits 3, 6 and 8.

$$\boxed{3} \quad \boxed{6} \quad \boxed{8}$$

Arrange them like this to make different multiplications:

$\bigcirc \cdot \bigcirc \times \bigcirc =$

a) What is the largest answer you can make?

b) What is the smallest answer you can make?

c) What answer is the nearest to 30?

How did you do?

Division

Learn and use these rules of divisibility.

A whole number is divisible, or can be divided exactly by:	
2 if the last digit is even, e.g. 34, 78, 136, 5100	**6** if it is even and the sum of its digits is divisible by 3, e.g. 816 (8 + 1 + 6 = 15) 714 (7 + 1 + 4 = 12)
3 if the sum of its digits can be divided by 3, e.g. 261 (2 + 6 + 1 = 9) 1005 (1 + 0 + 0 + 5 = 6)	**8** if the last three digits can be divided by 8, e.g. 7264 (264 ÷ 8 = 33) 19 432 (432 ÷ 8 = 54)
4 if the last two digits can be divided by 4, e.g. 508 (08 ÷ 4 = 2) 364 (64 ÷ 4 = 16) 9320 (20 ÷ 4 = 5)	**9** if the sum of its digits is divisible by 9, e.g. 675 (6 + 7 + 5 = 18) 2043 (2 + 0 + 4 + 3 = 9)
5 if the last digit is 0 or 5, e.g. 530, 105, 485	**10** if the last digit is 0, e.g. 580, 2630, 48 900

Warm up

1 Each of these numbers is exactly divisible by 9.

The last digit is missing. Write the missing digits.

a) 525__

b) 259__

c) 842__

d) 736__

e) 704__

f) 199__

2 Which numbers in this set can be divided exactly by **both** 3 and by 4?

324	507	928	684
610	291	756	396

3 Copy and write the numbers 2, 3, 4, 5, 6, 8, 9 or 10 in the correct spaces. Use the rules of divisibility to find the answers.

a) 96 is divisible by ____, ____, ____, ____ and ____.

b) 81 is divisible by ____ and ____.

c) 170 is divisible by ____, ____ and ____.

d) 156 is divisible by ____, ____, ____ and ____.

e) 1680 is divisible by ____, ____, ____, ____, ____, ____ and ____.

f) 4050 is divisible by ____, ____, ____, ____, ____ and ____.

Challenge yourself

4 Copy and complete the Venn diagram. Write these numbers in the correct sections. Which two of these numbers do not belong in the diagram?

| 2130 | 2004 | 5317 | 2790 | 3294 |

| 3700 | 5193 | 6219 | 6154 | 4815 |

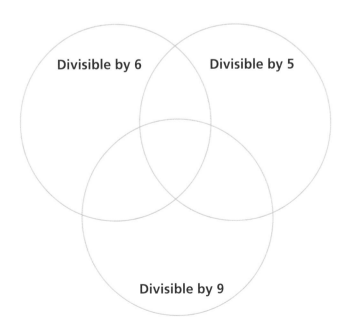

Divisible by 6   Divisible by 5

Divisible by 9

Progress test 1

1 $(24 \div 3) + 9 =$

2 Write six million two hundred and ten thousand and fifty as numerals.

3 $45 - (8 + 7) =$

4 Write < or > between these numbers to make this true.

925 059 ☐ 2 905 522

5 $(34 + 8) \div 6 =$

6 Copy the temperatures. Circle the lowest temperature and underline the highest temperature.

−12 °C   −2 °C   −20 °C

21 °C   −1 °C

7 $60 \div (3 \times 4) =$

8 Write the value of the underlined digit.

7 683 141

9 $(5 \times 9) - (36 - 12) =$

10 Copy the numbers. Circle the largest and underline the smallest number.

8 136 470   8 134 607

8 317 019   8 731 097   8 130 974

11 Copy and circle the digit with a value of **nine hundred**.

9 0 9 9 9 9 0

12 $6 \times (13 - 5) =$

13 Write < or > between these numbers to make this true.

10 ☐ −11

14 $(7 \times 3) + 54 =$

15 Write four million eight thousand one hundred and sixty as numerals.

16 $25 - (32 \div 4) =$

17 $(40 - 28) \times (27 \div 3) =$

Use this number line to help you answer questions 18–20.

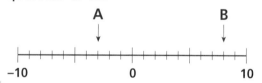

18 Write the number at each arrow.

19 What is the difference between −4 and −7?

20 What is the difference between −5 and 2?

Score ⬤/20

1 Multiply these.

$7 \times 5 =$

$0.7 \times 5 =$

2 $45 + 46 =$

3 Write the number that is exactly divisible by 9.

859 384 726

123 432

4 $238 - 93 =$

5 A cinema ticket costs £2.70.
What is the total cost of four tickets?

6 Will 6 divide exactly into 2 634?
Write Yes or No.

7 $0.9 \times 2 =$

8 Write the last digit of this four-digit number to make it exactly divisible by 8.

135

9 $72 - 15 =$

10 $183 + 52 =$

11 $579 - 36 =$

12 $10.4 \times 3 =$

13 Choose the numbers that will divide exactly into 234.

5 8

6 9

14 $127 + 19 =$

15 $0.8 \times 9 =$

16 What is 44p less than 81p?

17 $7.5 \times 8 =$

18 Which two numbers between 2052 and 2059 are divisible by 3?

19 A café serves 163 teas and 74 coffees in one day.
How many teas and coffees do they serve altogether?

20 $6.7 \times 6 =$

Score ⬤/20

Multiples and factors

Make sure you know the difference between **multiples** and **factors**.

Multiples

Multiples of any number can be divided exactly by that number. For example:

- 8, 12, 16, 20 and 24 are all multiples of 4.
- 12, 18, 24, 30 and 36 are all multiples of 6.

12 and 24 are **common multiples** of 4 and 6.

The **lowest common multiple** (LCM) of 4 and 6 is 12.

Factors

Factors are whole numbers that will divide exactly into other whole numbers. For example:

- The factors of 32 are (1, 32), (2, 16), (4, 8).
- The factors of 18 are (1, 18), (2, 9), (3, 6).

Numbers which are factors of two or more numbers are called **common factors**.

The common factors of 18 and 32 are 1 and 2.

The **highest common factor** (HCF) of 18 and 32 is 2.

Warm up

1. Find all the common multiples up to 99 for each pair of numbers.

    a) 3 and 5

    b) 6 and 10

    c) 4 and 9

    d) 2 and 5

2. Write the lowest common multiple for each pair of numbers in question 1.

3. Write the factors of these numbers in pairs.

    a) 48   **b)** 27   **c)** 45

    d) 36   **e)** 30   **f)** 42

4 What is the lowest common multiple for each of these?

　a) 6 and 8

　b) 9 and 5

　c) 2, 3 and 5

　d) 4, 9 and 6

　e) 6, 4 and 5

　f) 8, 3 and 2

5 Look at your answers for question 4. Use them to help you find the **common factors** for each of these.

　a) Common factors of 30 and 42

　b) Common factors of 27 and 45

　c) Common factors of 36 and 42

　d) Common factors of 42 and 48

　e) Common factors of 30 and 45

　f) Common factors of 27, 36 and 45

　g) Common factors of 36, 42 and 48

Now circle the **highest common factor** in each of your answers.

Challenge yourself

6 Write the following numbers on small squares of paper.

Place the numbers on this grid so they follow all the rules.

	Multiple of 3	Common factor of 20 and 30	Factor of 56
Odd number			
Common factor of 36 and 12			
> 4			

How did you do?

19

Squares and primes

Make sure you know what **square numbers** and **prime numbers** are.

Square numbers

The numbers 1, 4, 9 and 16 are examples of **square numbers**. Square numbers are found when two identical whole numbers are multiplied together, e.g.

3 squared = 9

4 squared = 16

$3^2 = 9$

$4^2 = 16$

Prime numbers

If a number only has two factors, itself and 1, then it is a **prime number**. For example, 17 is a prime number because it can only be divided exactly by 1 and 17.

The number 1 is not a prime number because it only has one factor – itself.

Warm up

1 Answer these.

a) $3 \times 3 = 3^2 =$

b) $10 \times 10 = 10^2 =$

c) $4 \times 4 = 4^2 =$

d) $6 \times 6 = 6^2 =$

e) $2^2 =$

f) $12^2 =$

g) $5^2 =$

h) $7^2 =$

i) $8^2 =$

j) $1^2 =$

k) $9^2 =$

l) $11^2 =$

Test yourself

2 Investigate the number of factors for each of the square numbers in question 1.

Copy and complete this sentence:

Square numbers always have an _____ number of factors.

3 Eratosthenes was a Greek mathematician who lived from 275 BC to 195 BC. He discovered a method of finding prime numbers of less than 100.

To use his method, follow the stages under the grid below:

1	2	3	4	5	6	7	8	9	10
11	12	13	14	15	16	17	18	19	20
21	22	23	24	25	26	27	28	29	30
31	32	33	34	35	36	37	38	39	40
41	42	43	44	45	46	47	48	49	50
51	52	53	54	55	56	57	58	59	60
61	62	63	64	65	66	67	68	69	70
71	72	73	74	75	76	77	78	79	80
81	82	83	84	85	86	87	88	89	90
91	92	93	94	95	96	97	98	99	100

a) Copy this number grid.

Cross out numbers using different colours:

- Cross out 1.
- Cross out all the multiples of 2, but not 2.
- Cross out all the multiples of 3, but not 3.
- Cross out all the multiples of 5, but not 5.
- Cross out all the multiples of 7, but not 7.

b) Write down all the numbers that you have not crossed out. If you have done it correctly, this will be a list of all the prime numbers to 100.

c) What do you notice about the factors of each of the numbers you have listed in part **b)**?

Equations and relationships

Equations have symbols or letters instead of numbers in a calculation.

For example, $\Delta + 5 = 18$ $4n - 2 = 18$ $3y + 6 = 21$

You can use the numbers given to help you work out the unknown symbol.

Example: $3y + 6 = 21$ **What is the value of y?**

You want y on one side of the equation and the numbers on the other.

Subtract 6 from both sides. If it was −6, you would add 6 to both sides.

$3y = 21 - 6$ $3y = 15$ $y = 5$

> *Remember that equations need to stay balanced. If you add, take away, multiply or divide a number from one side, do the same to the other side and the equation stays the same.*

A **formula** (plural is **formulae**) uses letters or words to give a rule.

Example: What is the rule for the relationship between A and B for each pair of numbers?

A	0	1	2	3	4	5	n
B	1	3	5	7	9	?	?

To work out B, you can double A then add 1: $B = 2A + 1$

So for n (or any number), the formula is $2n + 1$. You can use this to find any number in the sequence, so the 12th number is: $2 \times 12 + 1 = 25$

Warm up

1 What is the value of each letter in these equations?

a) $5c + 8 = 28$ **b)** $4y - 16 = 4$

c) $18 + 3p = 30$ **d)** $2r + 5 = 23$

e) $7a - 11 = 10$ **f)** $4w + 9 = 49$

Answers

Pages 4–5

1. a) 6 400 926   b) 9 218 074
   c) 2 100 000   d) 3 290 591
   e) 1 400 212   f) 4 001 390
   g) 7 002 008   h) 1 400 260
2. a) six million seven hundred and eighty-five thousand one hundred and forty-one
   b) one million five hundred and ten thousand nine hundred and thirty
3. a) 2(9)69 921
   b) 7 2(2)4 025
   c) (3)363 280
   d) 85(5)01 597
4.

City	Country	Population
Tokyo	Japan	35 521 740
Mexico City	Mexico	22 843 550
New York	USA	22 310 740
Mumbai	India	19 463 950
Shanghai	China	16 708 510
Cairo	Egypt	15 837 460
Moscow	Russia	14 432 190
London	UK	12 412 330

Pages 6–7

1. a) −17   b) −14   c) −6
   d) −1   e) 3   f) 9
2. a) 16   b) 9
   c) 23   d) 17
3. −14°C, −13°C, −5°C, 0°C, 3°C, 18°C
4. a) 6°   b) 45°   c) 21°
5. a) 1 m 6 cm (or 106 cm)   b) 93 cm (or 0.93 m)
   c) 6th attempt   d) 8th attempt
   e) 6 below the target (−6)

Pages 8–9

1. a) 18   b) 25
   c) 16   d) 43
   e) 33   f) 24
   g) 18   h) 6
2. a) (5 − 3) × (4 + 2) = 12
   b) 15 + (21 ÷ 7) − 8 = 10
   c) (9 ÷ 3) + (6 − 5) = 4
   d) 2 × (4 + 2) × 4 = 48
   e) (5 + 10) − (18 ÷ 9) = 13
3. a) 3   b) 2   c) 3
   d) 6   e) 3
4. There are many possible solutions. Check each calculation gives each number from 1–20 as the answer.

Pages 10–11

1. a) 145   b) 115
   c) 181   d) 183
   e) 223   f) 345
2. a) 26   b) 28
   c) 18   d) 76
   e) 67   f) 38
3. 3700 + 4800
   2900 + 5600
   3900 + 4600
4.

+	89	168
134	223	302
215	304	383

+	203	428
169	372	597
324	527	752

+	388	109
577	965	686
438	826	547

5. 495

Pages 12–13

1. a) 40, 4.0   b) 21, 2.1
   c) 36, 3.6   d) 42, 4.2
   e) 64, 6.4   f) 63, 6.3
   g) 49, 4.9   h) 45, 4.5
2. a) 20 + 1.5 = 21.5
   b) (7 × 8) + (0.5 × 8) = 56 + 4.0 = 60
   c) (8 × 9) + (0.6 × 9) = 72 + 5.4 = 77.4
   d) (5 × 3) + (0.9 × 3) = 15 + 2.7 = 17.7
   e) (6 × 7) + (0.2 × 7) = 42 + 1.4 = 43.4
3. a) 50.4   b) 20.4   c) 28.8

Pages 14–15

1. a) 6   b) 2
   c) 4   d) 2
   e) 7   f) 8
2. 324, 684, 756, 396
3. a) 2, 3, 4, 6 and 8
   b) 3 and 9
   c) 2, 5 and 10
   d) 2, 3, 4 and 6
   e) 2, 3, 4, 5, 6, 8 and 10
   f) 2, 3, 5, 6, 9 and 10
4.

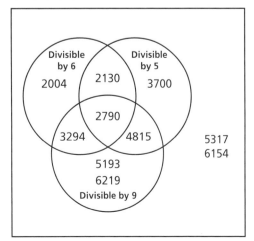

Answers

Page 16
1. 17
2. 6 210 050
3. 30
4. <
5. 7
6. (−20°C), 21°C
7. 5
8. six hundred thousand (or 600 000)
9. 21
10. (8 731 097), 8 130 974
11. 9 0 9 9 (9) 9 0
12. 48
13. >
14. 75
15. 4 008 160
16. 17
17. 108
18. −3, 8
19. 3
20. 7

Page 17
1. 35, 3.5
2. 91
3. 432
4. 145
5. £10.80
6. Yes
7. 1.8
8. 2
9. 57
10. 235
11. 543
12. 31.2
13. 6, 9
14. 146
15. 7.2
16. 37p
17. 60
18. 2055 and 2058
19. 237
20. 40.2

Pages 18–19
1. a) 15, 30, 45, 60, 75, 90   b) 30, 60, 90
   c) 36, 72
   d) 10, 20, 30, 40, 50, 60, 70, 80, 90
2. a) 15   b) 30   c) 36   d) 10
3. a) (1, 48) (2, 24) (3, 16) (4, 12) (6, 8)
   b) (1, 27) (3, 9)
   c) (1, 45) (3, 15) (5, 9)
   d) (1, 36) (2, 18) (3, 12) (4, 9) (6, 6)
   e) (1, 30) (2, 15) (3, 10) (5, 6)
   f) (1, 42) (2, 21) (3, 14) (6, 7)
4. a) 24   b) 45   c) 30   d) 36
   e) 60   f) 24
5. a) 1, 2, 3, (6)   b) 1, 3, (9)
   c) 1, 2, 3, (6)   d) 1, 2, 3, (6)
   e) 1, 3, 5, (15)   f) 1, 3, (9)
   g) 1, 2, 3, (6)
6. Several possible answers, including:

	Multiple of 3	Common factor of 20 and 30	Factor of 56
Odd number	3	1	7
Common factor of 36 and 12	6	2	4
> 4	9	5	8

Pages 20–21
1. a) 9   b) 100
   c) 16   d) 36
   e) 4   f) 144
   g) 25   h) 49
   i) 64   j) 1
   k) 81   l) 121
2. odd
3. a) Check all the numbers have been crossed out
      except those listed in **b)**.
   b) 2, 3, 5, 7, 11, 13, 17, 19, 23, 29, 31, 37, 41, 43,
      47, 53, 59, 61, 67, 71, 73, 79, 83, 89, 97
   c) Each number only has two factors, 1 and itself.

Pages 22–23
1. a) 4   b) 5
   c) 4   d) 9
   e) 3   f) 10
2. a) 10, $2n$
   b) 13, $2n + 3$
3. a) 31   b) 49
   c) 160   d) 5
   e) 2   f) 54
4. a) [$x = 1, y = 24$] [$x = 2, y = 12$] [$x = 3, y = 8$]
      [$x = 4, y = 6$] [$x = 6, y = 4$] [$x = 8, y = 3$]
      [$x = 12, y = 2$]
      [$x = 24, y = 1$]
   b) $x = 8, y = 3$

Pages 24–25
1. a) 6   b) 16
   c) 1   d) 3
   e) 5   f) 16
   g) 54   h) 10
   i) 9   j) 80
   k) 8   l) 7
2. a) <   b) <   c) <   d) <
   e) >   f) >   g) >   h) <
3. a) melons   b) James
   c) cup   d) non-fiction

Pages 26–27
1. a) 18, 56, 80, 60
   b) 32, 28, 84, 200
   c) 27, 69, 135, 81
   d) 63, 21, 77, 49
2. a) $2\frac{2}{3}$
   b) $2\frac{2}{5}$
   c) $2\frac{2}{4}$ (or $2\frac{1}{2}$)
   d) $6\frac{1}{2}$
   e) $1\frac{1}{2}$
   f) $3\frac{1}{3}$

3. a) £12
   b) 18
   c) 160 m
   d) 0.9 kg (or 900 g)
   e) 20

4. a) $\frac{3}{4}$ of 4.4 kg
   b) $\frac{7}{10}$ of 4 kg
   c) $\frac{3}{5}$ of 4.5 kg
   d) $\frac{3}{4}$ of 1.2 kg

Pages 28–29

1. a) $2\frac{7}{8}$ b) $1\frac{1}{10}$
   c) $1\frac{11}{15}$ d) $3\frac{19}{20}$
   e) $1\frac{3}{20}$ f) $4\frac{39}{40}$

2. a) $2\frac{1}{2}$ b) $3\frac{1}{9}$
   c) $1\frac{1}{5}$ d) $2\frac{13}{24}$
   e) $\frac{13}{20}$ f) $1\frac{1}{20}$

3. a) $2\frac{1}{20}$ b) $3\frac{7}{30}$
   c) $3\frac{27}{40}$ d) $3\frac{13}{15}$
   e) $1\frac{1}{4}$ f) $3\frac{3}{5}$

4. $\frac{1}{3} + \frac{1}{6} = \frac{1}{2}$
   $\frac{3}{10} + \frac{1}{5} = \frac{1}{2}$
   $\frac{3}{8} + \frac{1}{4} = \frac{5}{8}$

5. a) $\frac{3}{8}$ b) $\frac{1}{2}$
   c) $\frac{8}{15}$ d) $\frac{1}{12}$
   e) $\frac{3}{5}$ f) $\frac{1}{4}$

6. Various possible answers, all the fractions should total 1.

Page 30

1. (4, 8) 2. 72, 36
3. 25 4. 43
5. 28 6. 25
7. 16 8. 6
9. 72, 48 10. 36
11. 1, 3, 7, 21 12. 48
13. 3 14. 64
15. 23 16. 15
17. $3n$ 18. 121
19. 1, 3, 9 20. 12

Page 31

1. $\frac{6}{15}, \frac{6}{16}$ 2. Tuesday
3. 60 4. <
5. $3\frac{1}{8}$ 6. $\frac{3}{4}$ of 4.8 km
7. $4\frac{39}{40}$ 8. 14
9. $\frac{25}{35}, \frac{12}{16}$ 10. $\frac{5}{9} < \frac{4}{7} < \frac{2}{3}$
11. $\frac{3}{10}$ of 5 kg 12. $2\frac{3}{20}$
13. $1\frac{1}{6}$ 14. 27

15. 36 16. $4\frac{4}{5}$
17. > 18. $3\frac{43}{60}$
19. $\frac{3}{10}$ m 20. $\frac{9}{10}$ of the cake

Pages 32–33

1. a) 0.7 b) 0.9
   c) 0.4 d) 0.8
   e) 0.5 f) 0.75
   g) 0.45 h) 0.08
   i) 0.33 j) 0.09
   k) 0.63 l) 0.15

2. a) $\frac{1}{2}$ b) $\frac{3}{10}$
   c) $\frac{7}{10}$ d) $\frac{4}{5}$
   e) $\frac{2}{5}$ f) $\frac{21}{50}$
   g) $\frac{4}{25}$ h) $\frac{39}{50}$
   i) $\frac{17}{20}$

3. a) $4\frac{2}{10} = 4.2$ b) $9\frac{4}{10} = 9.4$
   c) $3\frac{8}{10} = 3.8$ d) $11\frac{6}{10} = 11.6$
   e) $4\frac{5}{10} = 4.5$ f) $3\frac{4}{100} = 3.04$
   g) $5\frac{78}{100} = 5.78$ h) $10\frac{6}{100} = 10.06$
   i) $6\frac{35}{100} = 6.35$

4. A $\frac{81}{100}$; 0.81 B $\frac{21}{25}$; 0.84 C $\frac{43}{50}$; 0.86
   D $\frac{87}{100}$; 0.87 E $\frac{22}{25}$; 0.88 F $\frac{89}{100}$; 0.89

5. a) $\frac{7}{100}, \frac{3}{10}, \frac{37}{100}, \frac{7}{10}$
   b) $\frac{41}{100}, \frac{1}{2}, \frac{3}{5}, \frac{7}{10}$
   c) $\frac{1}{50}, \frac{2}{25}, \frac{14}{50}, \frac{4}{5}$
   d) $\frac{29}{50}, \frac{18}{25}, \frac{3}{4}, \frac{4}{5}$

Pages 34–35

1. a) $\frac{1}{2} = 0.5 = 50\%$
   b) $\frac{1}{4} = 0.25 = 25\%$
   c) $\frac{1}{5} = 0.2 = 20\%$
   d) $\frac{2}{5} = 0.4 = 40\%$
   e) $\frac{17}{50} = 0.34 = 34\%$
   f) $\frac{7}{10} = 0.7 = 70\%$
   g) $\frac{7}{100} = 0.07 = 7\%$
   h) $\frac{11}{25} = 0.44 = 44\%$

2. a) $\frac{4}{5}$ b) $\frac{13}{25}$
   c) $\frac{3}{5}$ d) $\frac{17}{50}$
   e) $\frac{7}{20}$ f) $\frac{13}{20}$
   g) $\frac{1}{50}$ h) $\frac{49}{50}$

3. a) 70% b) 75%
   c) 80% d) 90%
   e) 60% f) 79%

4. a) Beth
   b) $\frac{45}{50}, \frac{4}{5}, \frac{79}{100}, \frac{15}{20}, \frac{7}{10}, \frac{15}{25}$

Answers

5. **a)** $\frac{3}{4}$ blue, $\frac{3}{20}$ red, $\frac{1}{20}$ white, $\frac{1}{20}$ yellow

b) $\frac{3}{5}$ blue, $\frac{3}{10}$ yellow, $\frac{2}{25}$ white, $\frac{1}{50}$ black

c) $\frac{11}{20}$ yellow, $\frac{1}{4}$ red, $\frac{9}{50}$ white, $\frac{1}{50}$ black

6. **a)** 1 litre   **b)** 1.6 litres   **c)** 3.6 litres

Pages 36–37

1.

What is?					
	10% of ...	20% of ...	5% of ...	50% of ...	25% of ...
£20	£2	£4	£1	£10	£5
£60	£6	£12	£3	£30	£15
£50	£5	£10	£2.50	£25	£12.50
£24	£2.40	£4.80	£1.20	£12	£6

2. **a)** £3, £9   **b)** £7, £28

c) £2.50, £7.50   **d)** £0.80, £0.40

e) £0.60, £1.20   **f)** £4, £48

3. **a)** Amount off: £4; New cost: £36

b) Amount off: £6; New cost: £54

c) Amount off: £14; New cost: £56

d) Amount off: £10; New cost: £15

e) Amount off: £4; New cost: £76

Pages 38–39

1. **a)** $\frac{1}{2}$ (or $\frac{3}{6}$)   **b)** $\frac{1}{2}$ (or $\frac{4}{8}$)

c) $\frac{7}{10}$ **d)** $\frac{2}{5}$

e) $\frac{3}{4}$ (or $\frac{6}{8}$)   **f)** $\frac{4}{5}$

2. **a)** 1 : 1   **b)** 1 : 1   **c)** 7 : 3

d) 2 : 3   **e)** 3 : 1   **f)** 4 : 1

3. **a)** 18   **b)** 3 : 1   **c)** 24

4. **a)** 300 g flour, 150 g butter, 100 g sugar, 50 g chocolate chips

b) 450 g flour, 225 g butter, 150 g sugar, 75 g chocolate chips

Pages 40–41

1. **a)** 90, 80, 80, 80, 70, 70, 60, 50, 50

b) 70   **c)** 80   **d)** 70

2. **a)** 140 cm   **b)** 140 cm   **c)** 150 cm

3. Median: 29 seconds; Mode: 28 seconds; Mean: 30 seconds

4. Median: 10 cm; Mode: 10 cm; Mean: 10 cm

Page 42

1. $\frac{3}{10}$, $\frac{4}{5}$ **2.** $\left(\frac{72}{100}\right)$, $\frac{2}{10}$

3. 0.2, 0.6   **4.** 0.5, 50%

5. $\frac{2}{5}$, $\frac{13}{50}$ **6.** $6\frac{8}{10}$ = 6.8, $7\frac{5}{10}$ = 7.5

7. 0.09, 9%   **8.** £3

9. $\frac{17}{20}$, $\frac{1}{4}$ **10.** £40

11. 0.25, 0.7   **12.** 0.4, 40%

13. £4.50   **14.** $\frac{9}{25}$, $\frac{57}{100}$

15. £4   **16.** $\frac{1}{20}$, $\frac{4}{25}$

17. 0.3, 0.09   **18.** $\left(\frac{4}{5}\right)$, $\frac{8}{100}$

19. 0.55, 55%   **20.** $1\frac{18}{100}$ = 1.18, $3\frac{55}{100}$ = 3.55

Page 43

1. 10   **2.** 100 g

3. 200 g   **4.** 1 : 3

5. 28   **6.** 30

7. 29   **8.** $\frac{1}{2}$

9. 1 : 1   **10.** $\frac{3}{4}$

11. 170 cm   **12.** 170 cm

13. 175 cm   **14.** 12°C

15. 12°C   **16.** 12°C

17. 5   **18.** 17

19. 16   **20.** mode

2 Write the value of *B* for each of these when *A* is 5.

Choose the correct rule for each relationship between *A* and *B*.

a)

A	0	1	2	3	4	5	n
B	0	2	4	6	8		?

$3n - 1$ $n + 1$ $2n$ $2n - 1$

b)

A	0	1	2	3	4	5	n
B	3	5	7	9	11		?

$4n$ $n + 3$ $3n + 1$ $2n + 3$

3 In an algebraic expression, letters are used as substitutes for numbers.

Find the value of the following expressions if $c = 5$ and $d = 8$.

a) $3c - d + 24 =$

b) $34 + 5(d - c) =$

c) $(84 - 4d) + (8c + 68) =$

d) $2(d + c) - 7(d - c) =$

e) $\dfrac{40}{d} - \dfrac{15}{c} =$

f) $6(4c - 2d) + 6c =$

4 The letters *x* and *y* stand for two whole numbers.

$$xy = 24$$

a) Which two numbers could *x* and *y* stand for? Write all the different possibilities in pairs, e.g. [x = ?, y = ?]

b) What if $xy = 24$ and $x - y = 5$?

How did you do?

Comparing fractions

It is easier to compare fractions if they have the same denominator.

If the denominators are not the same, you need to change them to equivalent fractions with a **common denominator**. To do this, you need to know the **lowest common multiple** for each denominator.

Example: Which is the larger fraction, $\frac{3}{5}$ or $\frac{3}{4}$?

First, change them to equivalent fractions.

The lowest common multiple of 5 and 4 is 20.

$$\overset{\times 4}{\frac{3}{5}} = \frac{12}{20} \qquad \overset{\times 5}{\frac{3}{4}} = \frac{15}{20}$$

$$\underset{\times 4}{} \qquad \underset{\times 5}{}$$

$\frac{15}{20} > \frac{12}{20}$ so $\frac{3}{4}$ is greater than $\frac{3}{5}$.

Warm up

1 Copy and complete the pairs of equivalent fractions.

a) $\frac{2}{3} = \frac{\square}{9}$

b) $\frac{5}{8} = \frac{10}{\square}$

c) $\frac{\square}{5} = \frac{2}{10}$

d) $\frac{1}{\square} = \frac{3}{9}$

e) $\frac{\square}{6} = \frac{30}{36}$

f) $\frac{4}{5} = \frac{\square}{20}$

g) $\frac{1}{9} = \frac{6}{\square}$

h) $\frac{7}{\square} = \frac{35}{50}$

i) $\frac{3}{11} = \frac{\square}{33}$

j) $\frac{7}{10} = \frac{56}{\square}$

k) $\frac{\square}{9} = \frac{24}{27}$

l) $\frac{6}{\square} = \frac{36}{42}$

2 Copy and complete with <, > or = between each pair of fractions.

Remember to change them to equivalent fractions.

a) $\frac{2}{3}$ ☐ $\frac{5}{6}$ b) $\frac{4}{7}$ ☐ $\frac{3}{4}$

c) $\frac{1}{3}$ ☐ $\frac{2}{5}$ d) $\frac{3}{8}$ ☐ $\frac{2}{5}$

e) $\frac{4}{5}$ ☐ $\frac{3}{4}$ f) $1\frac{5}{8}$ ☐ $1\frac{3}{10}$

g) $2\frac{7}{12}$ ☐ $2\frac{1}{2}$ h) $3\frac{3}{5}$ ☐ $3\frac{2}{3}$

Challenge yourself

3 Answer these problems.

a) A market trader has the same number of melons and pineapples to sell.
After an hour, $\frac{5}{8}$ of his melons are sold and $\frac{7}{12}$ of his pineapples are sold.
Which fruit has sold more?

b) James and Lizzie each had a bag of sweets with the same number of sweets
in each bag. James has $\frac{7}{10}$ of his sweets left and Lizzie has $\frac{5}{6}$ of her sweets left.
Who has eaten more sweets?

c) When United played City in the league, the stadium
was $\frac{3}{5}$ full. When they played each other in the cup,
later in the season, the stadium was $\frac{5}{8}$ full.
Which match had a bigger crowd – league or cup?

d) In a library there are fiction, non-fiction and poetry books. $\frac{7}{15}$ of the books are
non-fiction and $\frac{5}{12}$ of them are fiction.
Are there more fiction or non-fiction books?

Fractions of amounts

Finding fractions of quantities is very similar to dividing amounts.

Example: What is $\frac{2}{3}$ of 15?

$\frac{1}{3}$ of 15 = 15 ÷ 3 = 5

$\frac{2}{3}$ of 15 = 5 × 2 = 10 ⟵ *If the numerator is more than 1, divide the quantity by the denominator and then multiply by the numerator.*

Sometimes fractions of amounts leave fraction remainders.

Example: What is $\frac{1}{4}$ of 11?

$\frac{1}{4}$ of 11 = 2 remainder 3

$\frac{1}{4}$ of this remainder = $\frac{3}{4}$

$\frac{1}{4}$ of 11 = $2\frac{3}{4}$

Warm up

1 Complete each of these.

a) $\frac{2}{3}$ of…	b) $\frac{4}{5}$ of…	c) $\frac{3}{4}$ of…	d) $\frac{7}{10}$ of…
27 =	40 =	36 =	90 =
84 =	35 =	92 =	30 =
120 =	105 =	180 =	110 =
90 =	250 =	108 =	70 =

2 Answer these, writing each remainder as a fraction.

a)

$\frac{1}{3}$ of 8 =

b)

$\frac{1}{5}$ of 12 =

c)

$\frac{1}{4}$ of 10 =

d)

$\frac{1}{2}$ of 13 =

e)

$\frac{1}{8}$ of 12 =

f)

$\frac{1}{3}$ of 10 =

Challenge yourself

3 Answer these questions.

a) What is three-quarters of £16?

b) There are 27 children in a class and two-thirds are girls.
How many are girls?

c) What is four-fifths of 200 metres?

d) Three-fifths of the ingredients in a cake is flour. If the total weight of the cake is
1.5 kg, what is the weight of the flour used?

e) I am thinking of a number. Three-quarters of the number is 15.
What is the number I am thinking of?

4 Which of these is the heavier weight in each pair?

a) $\frac{2}{3}$ of 3.9 kg **or** $\frac{3}{4}$ of 4.4 kg

b) $\frac{7}{10}$ of 4 kg **or** $\frac{2}{3}$ of 3600 g

c) $\frac{3}{5}$ of 4.5 kg **or** $\frac{7}{10}$ of 2400 g

d) $\frac{3}{4}$ of 1.2 kg **or** $\frac{2}{5}$ of 1.5 kg

How did you do?

Fraction calculations

Fractions with different denominators are called **unlike fractions**. To add or subtract unlike fractions, you change them to like fractions by looking for equivalent fractions with a common denominator.

Follow these steps:

- Find equivalent fractions with a common denominator.

- Add the numerators and write the numerator over the common denominator.

- Simplify the fraction if needed.

Example: Add $\frac{1}{4}$ and $1\frac{2}{5}$.

Common denominator is 20.

$\frac{5}{20} + 1\frac{8}{20} = 1\frac{13}{20}$

Example: Subtract $\frac{1}{6}$ from $1\frac{2}{3}$.

Common denominator is 6.

$1\frac{4}{6} - \frac{1}{6} = 1\frac{3}{6} = 1\frac{1}{2}$

Example: $\frac{1}{2}$ of $\frac{1}{2}$ is $\frac{1}{4}$

This is the same as $\frac{1}{2} \times \frac{1}{2} = \frac{1}{4}$

To multiply fractions, multiply the numerators together and multiply the denominators together.

Warm up

1 Find the common denominator for the fractions in each addition. Write the answers in their simplest form.

a) $\frac{1}{8} + 2\frac{3}{4} =$

b) $\frac{4}{5} + \frac{3}{10} =$

c) $1\frac{2}{3} + \frac{1}{15} =$

d) $2\frac{7}{10} + 1\frac{1}{4} =$

e) $\frac{3}{4} + \frac{2}{5} =$

f) $4\frac{3}{5} + \frac{3}{8} =$

2 Find a common denominator and subtract these. Simplify your answers if needed.

a) $2\frac{4}{5} - \frac{3}{10} =$

b) $3\frac{2}{3} - \frac{5}{9} =$

c) $1\frac{1}{2} - \frac{3}{10} =$

d) $2\frac{7}{8} - \frac{1}{3} =$

e) $\frac{4}{5} - \frac{3}{20} =$

f) $2\frac{3}{4} - 1\frac{7}{10} =$

3 Read and answer these. Simplify your answers if needed.

a) What is $2\frac{3}{4}$ less than $4\frac{4}{5}$?

b) Subtract $3\frac{7}{15}$ from $6\frac{7}{10}$.

c) What is the difference between $2\frac{1}{5}$ and $5\frac{7}{8}$?

d) What is $4\frac{1}{5}$ take away $\frac{1}{3}$?

e) What is $5\frac{7}{20}$ subtract $4\frac{1}{10}$?

f) What is the difference between $4\frac{1}{2}$ and $\frac{9}{10}$?

4 Use each of the digits 1 to 6 once only to complete the equations below.

| **1** | **2** | **3** | **4** | **5** | **6** |

a) $\dfrac{\square}{3} + \dfrac{1}{\square} = \dfrac{1}{2}$

b) $\dfrac{\square}{10} + \dfrac{1}{5} = \dfrac{1}{\square}$

c) $\dfrac{3}{8} + \dfrac{1}{\square} = \dfrac{\square}{8}$

Challenge yourself

5 Answer these. Simplify each answer if needed.

a) $\frac{3}{4} \times \frac{1}{2} =$

b) $\frac{3}{4} \times \frac{2}{3} =$

c) $\frac{4}{5} \times \frac{2}{3} =$

d) $\frac{1}{3} \times \frac{1}{4} =$

e) $\frac{4}{5} \times \frac{3}{4} =$

f) $\frac{5}{12} \times \frac{3}{5} =$

6 Follow these instructions:

a) Draw four 6 × 4 square grids on squared paper.

b) Draw two straight lines to divide each grid into three unequal parts.

c) Divide each grid in a different way.

d) Write the unlike fractions of the grid in each part.

Example:

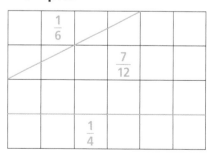

How did you do?

Progress test 3

1. Copy and write the missing pair of factors for 32.

   $32 \rightarrow$ (1, 32) (2, 16) (_____, _____)

2. Which numbers are multiples of both 2 and 9?

   ⟨27⟩ ⟨64⟩ ⟨36⟩
   ⟨72⟩ ⟨45⟩

3. $5^2 =$

4. Choose the prime number.

   ⟨39⟩ ⟨43⟩ ⟨33⟩
   ⟨21⟩ ⟨15⟩

5. What is the lowest common multiple of 4 and 7?

6. What is the missing factor for 50?

   1, 2, 5, 10 , _____, 50

7. Calculate this, when $p = 4$ and $m = 8$.

   $5m - 6p =$

8. What does t equal in this equation?

   $6t - 16 = 20$

9. Choose the numbers that are multiples of both 6 and 8.

   ⟨42⟩ ⟨72⟩ ⟨48⟩
   ⟨56⟩ ⟨36⟩

10. $6^2 =$

11. What are the common factors of 42 and 21?

12. Calculate this, when $j = 7$ and $k = 3$.

    $5(j - k) + 4j =$

13. What does d equal in this equation?

    $25 + 7d = 46$

14. $8^2 =$

15. What is the next prime number after 19?

Look at this chart for questions 16–17.

A	0	1	2	3	4	5	n
B	0	3	6	9	12		?

16. What is the value of B when A is 5?

17. Choose the correct rule for the relationship between A and B.

    $n + 3$ $3n$ $2n + 1$ $4n - 1$

18. $11^2 =$

19. What are the common factors of 18, 9 and 27?

20. What is the lowest common multiple of 4, 3 and 6?

Score ⬤/ 20

1 Copy and complete these equivalent fractions.

$\frac{2}{5} = \frac{\square}{15}$

$\frac{3}{8} = \frac{6}{\square}$

2 Amy reads $\frac{3}{10}$ of her book on Monday and $\frac{2}{5}$ of the book on Tuesday.

On which day does she read most?

3 $\frac{3}{10}$ of 200 =

4 Copy and write < or > between this pair of fractions.

$\frac{1}{4}$ $\square$ $\frac{4}{7}$

5 Answer this, writing the remainder as a fraction.

$\frac{1}{8}$ of 25 =

6 Which is the longer distance?

$\frac{1}{2}$ of 5.6 km $\frac{3}{4}$ of 4.8 km

7 $\frac{3}{5} + 4\frac{3}{8} =$

8 What is two-thirds of 21?

9 Copy and complete these equivalent fractions.

$\frac{5}{7} = \frac{\square}{35}$

$\frac{3}{4} = \frac{12}{\square}$

10 Write these fractions in order, starting with the smallest.

$\frac{2}{3}$ $\frac{5}{9}$ $\frac{4}{7}$

11 Which is the heavier weight?

$\frac{3}{10}$ of 5 kg $\frac{2}{5}$ of 3 kg

12 What is $\frac{3}{4}$ less than $2\frac{9}{10}$?

13 $2\frac{5}{6} - 1\frac{2}{3} =$

14 A necklace has 36 beads and three-quarters are blue. How many beads are blue?

15 $\frac{3}{5}$ of 60 =

16 Answer this, writing the remainder as a fraction.

$\frac{1}{5}$ of 24 =

17 Copy and write < or > between this pair of fractions.

$\frac{2}{3}$ $\square$ $\frac{3}{5}$

18 $2\frac{3}{10} + 1\frac{5}{12} =$

19 Lee can throw a ball $3\frac{4}{5}$ m and Ben can throw a ball $3\frac{1}{2}$ m. How much further can Lee throw a ball than Ben?

20 Which is the larger slice of cake?

$\frac{9}{10}$ of the cake $\frac{5}{6}$ of the cake

Score ⬤/ 20   31

Fractions and decimals

To change fractions to decimals, change them to tenths or hundredths.

This number line is divided into tenths. They are written as common fractions and decimal fractions.

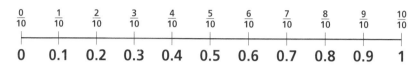

Example:

$\frac{1}{10} = 0.1$ zero point one

$\frac{2}{10} = 0.2$ zero point two

$\frac{2}{10}$ can be simplified to $\frac{1}{5}$, so $\frac{1}{5}$ is equal to 0.2

There are fractions and decimals between tenths.

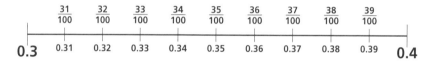

Example:

$\frac{31}{100} = 0.31$ zero point three one

$\frac{32}{100} = 0.32$ zero point three two

$\frac{32}{100}$ can be simplified to $\frac{8}{25}$, so $\frac{8}{25}$ is equal to 0.32

Warm up

1 Write these as decimals.

a) $\frac{7}{10}$ =   b) $\frac{9}{10}$ =   c) $\frac{2}{5}$ =

d) $\frac{4}{5}$ =   e) $\frac{50}{100}$ =   f) $\frac{75}{100}$ =

g) $\frac{45}{100}$ =   h) $\frac{8}{100}$ =   i) $\frac{33}{100}$ =

j) $\frac{9}{100}$ =   k) $\frac{63}{100}$ =   l) $\frac{15}{100}$ =

2 Write these as fractions. Simplify them if possible.

a) 0.5 =   b) 0.3 =   c) 0.7 =

d) 0.8 =   e) 0.4 =   f) 0.42 =

g) 0.16 =   h) 0.78 =   i) 0.85 =

3 Copy and change these to tenths or hundredths and write them as decimal fractions.

a) $4\frac{1}{5}$ =   b) $9\frac{2}{5}$ =   c) $3\frac{4}{5}$ =

d) $11\frac{3}{5}$ =   e) $4\frac{1}{2}$ =   f) $3\frac{1}{25}$ =

g) $5\frac{39}{50}$ =   h) $10\frac{3}{50}$ =   i) $6\frac{7}{20}$ =

4 Write the missing numbers A–F as fractions and decimals. Simplify the fractions if possible.

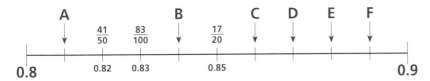

5 Write each set in order, starting with the smallest.

a)

| $\frac{3}{10}$ | $\frac{7}{10}$ | $\frac{7}{100}$ | $\frac{37}{100}$ |

b)

| $\frac{1}{2}$ | $\frac{3}{5}$ | $\frac{7}{10}$ | $\frac{41}{100}$ |

c)

| $\frac{2}{25}$ | $\frac{14}{50}$ | $\frac{4}{5}$ | $\frac{1}{50}$ |

d)

| $\frac{4}{5}$ | $\frac{29}{50}$ | $\frac{18}{25}$ | $\frac{3}{4}$ |

How did you do?   ☺ 😐 ☹

Fractions, decimals and percentages

It is easy to convert between percentages and decimals.

per cent to decimal

Divide the percentage by 100, e.g.

40% is the same as 0.4

decimal to per cent

Multiply the decimal by 100, e.g.

0.35 is the same as 35%

When you convert from fractions to percentages, you may find it easier to write the fraction as a decimal and then multiply by 100.

For example, $\frac{3}{4}$ is 0.75, which is the same as 75%.

Warm up

1 Copy and complete these.

a) $\dfrac{1}{\square} = 0.\_\_\_ = 50\%$

b) $\dfrac{\square}{4} = 0.25 = \_\_\_\%$

c) $\dfrac{1}{5} = 0.\_\_\_ = \_\_\_\%$

d) $\dfrac{2}{\square} = 0.4 = \_\_\_\%$

e) $\dfrac{17}{50} = 0.\_\_\_ = \_\_\_\%$

f) $\dfrac{7}{\square} = 0.7 = \_\_\_\%$

g) $\dfrac{\square}{100} = 0.07 = \_\_\_\%$

h) $\dfrac{11}{\square} = 0.44 = \_\_\_\%$

Test yourself

2 Write each of these percentages as a fraction reduced to its simplest form.

a) 80% =

b) 52% =

c) 60% =

d) 34% =

e) 35% =

f) 65% =

g) 2% =

h) 98% =

3 Copy and change these test scores to percentages.

a) Adam: $\frac{7}{10}$ = _____%

b) Ben: $\frac{15}{20}$ = _____%

c) Anna: $\frac{4}{5}$ = _____%

d) Beth: $\frac{45}{50}$ = _____%

e) Asif: $\frac{15}{25}$ = _____%

f) Claire: $\frac{79}{100}$ = _____%

Name	Score	Percentage

4 Look at the results in question 3.

a) Which child has the highest percentage score?

b) Write the test scores in order, starting with the highest.

Challenge yourself

5 These are the percentages of colours used to mix different paints. Convert the percentages to fractions in their simplest form.

a)

75% blue =

15% red =

5% white =

5% yellow =

b)

60% blue =

30% yellow =

8% white =

2% black =

c)

55% yellow =

25% red =

18% white =

2% black =

6 If the paint tins are 20 litres in size, how many litres of white paint are used in each tin?

How did you do?

Percentages

Look at the following percentage question: **What is 20% of £40?**

Try these two methods to solve this type of percentage question.

Method 1

Change to a fraction and work it out:

$20\% = \frac{20}{100} = \frac{1}{5}$

$\frac{1}{5}$ of £40 = £40 ÷ 5

$\quad\quad\quad = £8$

Method 2

Use 10% to work it out – just divide the number by 10:

10% of £40 is £4

So, 20% of £40 is double that: £8

Warm up

1 Copy and complete this table.

	What is?				
	10% of ...	**20% of ...**	**5% of ...**	**50% of ...**	**25% of ...**
£20	£2				
£60			£3		
£50		£10			
£24					£6

2 Write the percentages of each of these amounts.

a) £30

10% = £ _____

30% = £ _____

b) £70

10% = £ _____

40% = £ _____

c) £25

10% = £ _____

30% = £ _____

d) £8

10% = £ _____

5% = £ _____

e) £60

1% = £ _____

2% = £ _____

f) £400

1% = £ _____

12% = £ _____

Challenge yourself

3 In a sale everything is reduced in price. Write the amount taken off and the new cost of each item. Remember to subtract the percentage of the price from the original price.

a)    Was £40 ⟶ Now 10% off

b)    Was £60 ⟶ Now reduced by 10%

c)    Was £70 ⟶ 20% discount today

d)   Was £25 ⟶ Special offer 40% off

e)    Was £80 ⟶ Now reduced by 5%

How did you do?

Ratio and proportion

Ratio compares one amount with another.

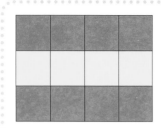

Example: What is the ratio of yellow to red tiles?

For every one yellow tile, there are two red tiles.
The ratio of yellow to red is 1 to 2, written as 1 : 2.

This ratio stays the same for any number of tiles arranged in this way:

Yellow	1	2	3	4	5	6
Red	2	4	6	8	10	12

Working out the **proportion** is the same as finding the fraction of the whole amount. The proportion of yellow tiles is 4 out of 12, which is one in every three or $\frac{1}{3}$.

Two quantities are in **direct proportion** when they increase or decrease in the same ratio.

Example: If three drinks cost £1.20, what is the cost of 15 drinks?

This is five times the number of drinks, so it is five times the price.

£1.20 × 5 = £6

Warm up

1 Look at these tile patterns. What proportion of each of the patterns is blue?

a)

b)

c)

d)

e)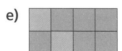

f)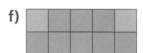

2 Write the ratio of blue to green tiles for each pattern in question 1.

3 Read and answer these.

a) In a class there are two girls to every three boys.

There are 30 children in the class. How many boys are there?

b) A 200 g snack bar has 75% oats and 25% fruit.

What is the ratio of oats to fruit in a bar, in its simplest form?

c) Dan mixes 1 litre of white paint with every 4 litres of blue paint. He needs 30 litres of paint altogether.

How many litres of blue paint will he need?

Challenge yourself

4 In this recipe, the amount of each ingredient is given as a proportion of the total weight.

a) What are the weights of each ingredient?

600 g Chocolate Chip Cookies
$\frac{1}{2}$ flour = ____ g
$\frac{1}{4}$ butter = ____ g
$\frac{1}{6}$ sugar = ____ g
$\frac{1}{12}$ chocolate chips = ____ g

b) Using this recipe, what weight of each ingredient would be needed for 900 g of cookies?

flour = ____ g   butter = ____ g

sugar = ____ g   chocolate chips = ____ g

How did you do?

Mean, mode and median

Mode, median and mean are three types of average.

Mode is the most common number.

Median is the middle number when listed in order. When there is an even number of items, the median is the midpoint between the **two** middle numbers.

Mean is the total of all the numbers divided by the number of items.

Example: This chart shows the goals scored by five players in a football team. What are the mode, median and mean for the number of goals scored?

Player	Alex	Billy	Chris	David	Eric
Goals scored	8	4	8	6	9

Mode: Two players scored **8** goals, so that is the mode.

Median: 4, 6, **8**, 8, 9

So 8 is the median number of goals.

Mean: 4 + 6 + 8 + 8 + 9 = 35   35 ÷ 5 = 7

So the mean is 7 goals.

Warm up

1 These are the results of a maths test out of 100 for a group of nine children:

80   60   70   70   80   50   50   80   90

a) Write the scores in order, starting with the highest.

b) What is the median score?

c) Which score is the mode?

d) Calculate the mean score.

2 These are the heights of a group of five children:

150 cm   140 cm   130 cm   140 cm   190 cm

a) Which height is the mode?

b) What is the median height?

c) What is the mean height?

3 These are the times taken to run 200 metres by a group of athletes.

Write the median, mode and mean times.

Name	Time (seconds)
Anna	28
Jo	34
Sally	29
Grace	28
Jasmine	31

Challenge yourself

4 These are the hand-spans for a group of 10 children.

What are the median, mode and mean hand-spans for this group?

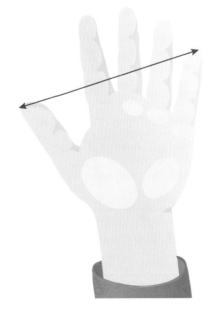

13 cm	11 cm
9 cm	10 cm
10 cm	8 cm
12 cm	9 cm
8 cm	10 cm

How did you do?

1 Write these decimals as fractions. Simplify them if possible.

0.3 =

0.8 =

2 Copy the fractions. Circle the largest and underline the smallest fraction.

$\frac{27}{100}$ $\frac{7}{10}$ $\frac{2}{10}$ $\frac{72}{100}$

3 Write these fractions as decimals.

$\frac{1}{5}$ =

$\frac{3}{5}$ =

4 Write this fraction as a decimal and a percentage.

$\frac{1}{2}$ = _____ • _____ = _____ %

5 Write these percentages as fractions. Simplify them if possible.

40% =

26% =

6 Change these mixed numbers to tenths or hundredths and write them as decimal fractions.

$6\frac{4}{5} = \frac{\square}{\square}$ = _____ • _____

$7\frac{1}{2} = \frac{\square}{\square}$ = _____ • _____

7 Write this fraction as a decimal and a percentage.

$\frac{9}{100}$ = _____ • _____ = _____ %

8 5% of £60 = £ _____

9 Write these decimals as fractions. Simplify them if possible.

0.85 =

0.25 =

10 In a sale there is 20% off a chair at £50. What is the sale price of the chair?

11 Write these decimal fractions as decimals.

$\frac{25}{100}$ =

$\frac{70}{100}$ =

12 Write this fraction as a decimal and a percentage.

$\frac{2}{5}$ = _____ • _____ = _____ %

13 15% of £30 = £ _____

14 Write these decimals as fractions. Simplify them if possible.

0.36 =

0.57 =

15 25% of £16 = £ _____

16 Write these percentages as fractions. Simplify them if possible.

5% =

16% =

17 Write these fractions as decimals.

$\frac{3}{10}$ =

$\frac{9}{100}$ =

18 Copy the fractions. Circle the largest and underline the smallest fraction.

$\frac{7}{10}$ $\frac{3}{4}$ $\frac{4}{5}$ $\frac{8}{100}$

19 Write this fraction as a decimal and a percentage.

$\frac{11}{20}$ = _____ • _____ = _____ %

20 Change these mixed numbers to tenths or hundredths and write them as decimal fractions.

$1\frac{9}{50} = \frac{\square}{\square}$ = _____

$3\frac{11}{20} = \frac{\square}{\square}$ = _____

Score ⬤ / 20

Progress test 6

1 To make concrete two bags of cement are mixed with five bags of stones. If I use four bags of cement, how many bags of stones will I need?

> The ratio for making pastry is 1 : 2, butter to flour. Now answer questions 2 and 3.

2 If 50 g of butter is used, how much flour will be needed?

3 How much butter is needed if 400 g of flour is used?

4 A 400 ml carton has 25% juice and 75% water. What is the ratio of juice to water in the carton, in its simplest form?

> These are the numbers of children in each class in a school. Write the average class sizes for questions 5–7.
>
> 32   28   29   28   33

5 Which class size is the mode?

6 What is the mean class size?

7 What is the median class size?

8 What proportion of this pattern is red?

9 What is the ratio of red to white tiles above?

10 A 300 g apple pie is made with 75% apples and 25% pastry. What is the proportion of apples in the pie, in its simplest form?

> These are the lengths of seven skipping ropes. Now answer questions 11–13.
>
> 170 cm   165 cm   170 cm
> 170 cm   190 cm   195 cm   165 cm

11 What is the median length?

12 What length is the mode?

13 What is the mean length?

> These are the temperatures over one week in March. Write the average temperatures for questions 14–16.
>
> 15°C   13°C   9°C   12°C
>   12°C   12°C   11°C

14 Mode: _____°C

15 Mean: _____°C

16 Median: _____°C

17 If you buy eight pencils, you get a free sharpener. If a teacher buys 40 pencils, how many sharpeners will she get free?

> Look at these spelling test scores for Ross then answer questions 18 and 19.
>
> **Monday 19   Tuesday 14**
> **Wednesday 17   Thursday 18**

18 What is his mean score?

19 On Friday he got 12 in the spelling test. What is his mean score now?

20 In a shoe shop they need to stock the size of shoe that sells the most. Would it be better to calculate the mean, mode or median average for this task?

Score ⬤/20

Published by Keen Kite Books
An imprint of HarperCollins*Publishers* Ltd
1 London Bridge Street
London SE1 9GF

ISBN 9780008161255

Text © 2013 Paul Broadbent and © 2015 Keen Kite Books,
an imprint of HarperCollins*Publishers* Ltd

Design © 2015 Keen Kite Books,
an imprint of HarperCollins*Publishers* Ltd